# LOOSE CANON

### SIX SHORT PLAYS BY
## BRIAN RENO
### AND
## GABRIEL VEGA WEISSMAN

★

DRAMATISTS
PLAY SERVICE
INC.

**SPECIAL NOTE**

Anyone receiving permission to produce LOOSE CANON is required to give credit to the Authors as sole and exclusive Authors of the Play on the title page of all programs distributed in connection with performances of the Play and in all instances in which the title of the Play appears, including printed or digital materials for advertising, publicizing or otherwise exploiting the Play and/or a production thereof. Please see your production license for font size and typeface requirements.

Be advised that there may be additional credits required in all programs and promotional material. Such language will be listed under the "Additional Billing" section of production licenses. It is the licensee's responsibility to ensure any and all required billing is included in the requisite places, per the terms of the license.

**SPECIAL NOTE ON SONGS AND RECORDINGS**

Dramatists Play Service, Inc. neither holds the rights to nor grants permission to use any songs or recordings mentioned in the Play. Permission for performances of copyrighted songs, arrangements or recordings mentioned in this Play is not included in our license agreement. The permission of the copyright owner(s) must be obtained for any such use. For any songs and/or recordings mentioned in the Play, other songs, arrangements, or recordings may be substituted provided permission from the copyright owner(s) of such songs, arrangements or recordings is obtained; or songs, arrangements or recordings in the public domain may be substituted.

*Dedicated to Moira and Robert Reno*
*&*
*Rosa and Andrew Weissman*

LOOSE CANON had its world premiere at the Scranton Shakespeare Festival (Michael Bradshaw Flynn, Artistic Director) on July 17th, 2015. It was directed by Logan Reed. The company was comprised of Becky Baumwoll, Grant Chamberlin, Cynthia Nesbit, Todd Rizley, Tamara Sevunts, and Daniel Tepper.

LOOSE CANON was produced at the New York International Fringe Festival (Nicole Dancel, Producer) on August 16th, 2015. It was directed by Logan Reed. The scenic and prop designs were by Riw Rakkulchon, the costume design was by Ntokozo F. Kunene, the lighting design was by Zach Blane, and the sound design was by Zack McKenna. The stage manager was Valerie Insardi. The company was comprised of Becky Baumwoll, Grant Chamberlin, Cynthia Nesbit, Todd Rizley, Tamara Sevunts, and Daniel Tepper.

LOOSE CANON was subsequently produced at SoHo Playhouse for the New York International Fringe Festival Encore Series (Nicole Dancel and Showgofa Hamraz, Producers) on October 19th, 2015. It was directed by Logan Reed. The scenic and prop designs were by Riw Rakkulchon, the costume design was by Ntokozo F. Kunene, the lighting design was by Zach Blane, and the sound design was by Emma Wilk. The stage manager was Valerie Insardi. The company was comprised of Grant Chamberlin, Cynthia Nesbit, Todd Rizley, Tamara Sevunts, Daniel Tepper, and Alli Trussell.

# ACKNOWLEDGMENTS

The playwrights would like to thank:

Mary Jo and Ted Shen for sponsoring the first public reading as well as the company from that reading: Melis Aker, Greg Brostom, Kyle Cameron, Holly Chou, Alexa Chryssos, Raviv Ullman, and Sophie Lewis.

Michael Bradshaw Flynn and the Scranton Shakespeare Festival.

Our company and designers from the Scranton and New York City productions as well as those behind the scenes: Nicole Dancel and Showgofa Hamraz, Samantha Kindler, Lisa Goldberg, Lily Robinson, Anna Haczkiewicz, Leah DeGruchy, and Katherine Banos.

Logan Reed for helming the first productions and teaching us so much about these plays.

# AUTHORS' NOTE

*Loose Canon* was written largely as an exploration of language and different styles of playwriting through the ages. The plays in this collection were conceived with great admiration for the playwrights being parodied, and with a desire to investigate how their distinct styles permeate contemporary theater. They are not meant to insult or deride. Familiarity with the playwrights on whose work *Loose Canon* is based is not obligatory, but investigating those playwrights will only enrich your production.

# NOTE ON CASTING

*Loose Canon* was developed with a company of six actors—three male and three female—in mind. However, it can be produced for a bigger company; role doubling is not essential. Similarly, the roles can be cast with an uneven gender split, with actors of all shapes, sizes, races, and gender identities. These roles are for everyone.

With regard to the characters in "The El Taqueria": While the characters are specifically not Hispanic, they can be played by anyone. Please do not avoid casting Latinx actors in these roles.

# CONTENTS

# THE ELMAE
## (Inspired by the works of Euripides)

# CHARACTERS

JASON

&

## CHORUS:

CHORUS LEADER

TIRESIAS

CASSANDRA

HECTOR

HELEN


## SETTING

A suburban Chuck E. Cheese's. 1996.

It is Jason's 5th birthday party.
The party guests make up the Chorus.

# THE ELMAE

*The Chorus enters led by the Chorus Leader, who stands in the center. They are wearing elaborate masks made out of papier mâché, macaroni, and other arts and crafts supplies. When they finish taking their positions, they remove the masks.*

CHORUS LEADER.
> It is January of 1996. Christmas is but two weeks passed.
> Gloom has again sunk its blunt talons into our wearied souls.
> And it is now, in this melancholy,
> That we gather in this dilapidated Chuck E. Cheese's
> To celebrate our friend Jason's birthday.

CHORUS.
> Oh the holidays. Trees indoors, stockings hung over fires,
> The sweet, sweet taste of cookies and candies and Jelly Bellys.

HELEN.
> Only days ago did fine aromas drift from our mothers' kitchens,
> Dishes brought forth from their holiday conviviality.

HECTOR.
> And see our fathers, who often stay too long a' work,
> Their keys jangling as they enter with a tray of Ferrero Rocher.

CHORUS.
> But that was the holidays and the holidays are no more.

CASSANDRA.
> And our fathers come home,
> Moments before bedtime, just long enough to
> Perfume us with whiskey, bar nuts, and despair.

CHORUS LEADER.
> Jason's birthday is a trying birthday,
> For we've all just received our presents not but a week ago,
> And now have to watch as our parents hand over

More presents that should have been ours,
Placing them into the lap of that dough-faced fool.

CHORUS.

It's a sham.

CHORUS LEADER.

The tokens have all been slotted and the tickets redeemed,

HELEN.

The Skee balls have been shot

TIRESIAS.

And the moles have all been whackéd.

CHORUS LEADER.

The cake, Costco-bought and soggy,
Has been de-flamed and consumed.
It is now time to put on our cheery facade
And watch Jason open his gifts.

*Jason steps out.*

JASON.

Welcome, Friends, and behold, as I take each of your perfectly
Wrapped, tinseled, tailored parcels and… just tear 'em up.

*He begins to unwrap presents.*

CHORUS LEADER.

A 96-color Crayola kit is essential to an emerging
Kindergartner, but lacking slush gray, sludge brown,
And dirty white we are incapable of completing
Our winter scenes coloring books.
It's useless.

CHORUS.

Useless.

JASON.

Many thanks, Cassandra. Now I can replace my nubs!
I wonder what this could be?

*He begins to open another gift.*

Splendid, a Playskool Toolkit! Thanks, Helen.

CHORUS LEADER.

Helen, were you given a Playskool Toolkit for Christmas?

*She shakes her head no.*

CHORUS.

Typical.

CHORUS LEADER.
> Mom buys a wondrous gift for someone else's rugrat,
> And shafts poor Helen with a "So You Think You Can Read"
> Deck of flashcards.

CHORUS.
> We are not interested in clearance-bin stocking stuffers.
> We want gifts that will prepare us for our future.

HECTOR.
> How can a man protect his hearth and home without a
> Nerf Max Force BallZooka?

HELEN.
> Without an Easy-Bake Oven, how can a woman learn to make
> Peach cobbler with a lightbulb?

> *Jason picks up a present wrapped in gorgeous, ornate wrapping paper.*

JASON.
> What's this? There's no note, no card...

> *Jason unwraps a Tickle Me Elmo. The Chorus gasps. Beat. Tiresias takes a step out.*

TIRESIAS.
> What is it?

CHORUS.
> Oh, Tiresias, if only you could see...
> It's the greatest toy ever to be had.
> A Tickle Me Elmo.
> No one, rich or poor, gifted or stunted, could
> Get one this Christmas.
> His soft red fur invited you to rub his tummy—
> But if you even get close to tickling him...

TIRESIAS.
> I know what a Tickle Me Elmo is!

CHORUS LEADER.
> Poor Tiresias. Born without the gift of sight.
> Lives above *Spanakopia*! The sketchy, grade-B
> Greek dinner theater on the south side of town.

TIRESIAS.
> I can hear you!
> And though my eyes might fail me, my sight does not.

We need to proceed to the next gift.
Only evil can come from this present!

CASSANDRA.
> He's right! Let this be.
> You'll see, we won't even care about Elmo in a few years' time.
> We'll be on to a boy… crammed… under a staircase…
> With a scar in the shape of a lightning bolt…

> *Beat. They all burst into hysterical laughter.*

CHORUS LEADER. *(Recovering from laughing.)*
> You crack me up, Cassandra.
> Every day coming up with this crazy stuff.
> Talking about some deformed child…
> Why don't you take a nap or something…

> *Beat.*

JASON.
> Oh Joy! Oh ecstasy! Sweet Elmo, like you,
> An incurable happiness has been lodged in my chest.
> Two double-A batteries of joy possess my soul and now
> My world is red… and furry.

CHORUS.
> Jason, what a beautiful present.
> May we each have a turn tickling your Elmo?

JASON.
> Haha—maybe later.
> But there are still more presents to open.

CHORUS LEADER.
> Come now, Jason, we're all your friends gathered for this party,
> Show some amicable spirit.

CHORUS.
> Let us have a tickle.

TIRESIAS.
> Let this be! I beg of you. Don't partake in the tickling.
> We must move past this. Jason, you must have another present
> You are dying to open.

CHORUS LEADER.
> NO! Jason is the only child with the famed Tickle Me Elmo.
> He must give us a chance to gently nuzzle the tips of
> Our fingers into Elmo's plush belly!

JASON.

Well, to be honest, between the Costco cake and all that Gak,
I don't want any of your grubby little fingers
Marring my sweet Elmo's coat.

CHORUS LEADER.

Your greed astounds us.

JASON.

Greed?! I don't see greediness.
In fact, this is the most generous I've ever felt.
You all can have whatever gifts you want.
Here Helen, have a Wacky Noodle. On me. Sorry.
Hector. Here why don't you take this one. You can even open it.

*He hands out gifts opened and unopened to members of the
Chorus.*

There! Now everyone goes home happy from my birthday party!

CHORUS LEADER.

There are no words to describe how disappointed we are.
That charming red monster you hold in your arms
Has given us hope that there is more to this life
Than chicken pox and early onset type 2 diabetes.
He has given us joy, education, music, laughter—
And here he is now, made flesh and cloth for all of us to worship.
We, more than any other generation, are the followers of Elmo.
We are the Elmae.
You have denied us.

JASON.

This is MY Birthday. This is MY special day.
IT'S MY PARTY. MINE. MIIIIIIIINE! It's my day and clearly
If I got an Elmo it means that I'm more special than
Any of you chumps. Look at you. You're disgusting.
Dressed in your OshKosh B'gosh best. Kissing butt
So you can be the one sitting next to the birthday boy!
Pathetic. Now I have Elmo. He's all I need.
LAUGH ELMO, LAUGH!!!

*He tickles—Elmo laughs, then Jason laughs maniacally.*

CHORUS.

GET THE TOY!!!

*Pandemonium breaks out. Gifts are violently unwrapped, toys
are broken, lots of screaming. Someone cries "MY PULL-UPS*

*MY PULL-UPS!" The chaos results in characters creating tableaus from famous Greek plays. Mostly with limbs of stuffed animals: Medea carrying her children's bodies; Agave carrying Pentheus' head. A female member of the Chorus holds up a sign reading "Girls Unite! Withhold Hugs and Kisses until Jason shares the Elmo!" Endless possibilities!*

TIRESIAS.
WAIT!

> *Chaos subsides to reveal Elmo on the ground, gargling tickle noises, and then silence. Jason weeps, picks up the doll.*

JASON. *(Quietly.)*
Oh gods, oh gods
If only I shared…

> *Jason slowly walks offstage, Chorus follows. Cassandra and Tiresias remain.*

TIRESIAS.
We tried, we tried to warn them…
CASSANDRA.
We always do, and they never listen…

> *Tiresias extends his hand to be taken by Cassandra so she can guide him off. She begins to walk off before realizing and coming back to help him.*

## End of Play

# PROPERTY LIST

Wrapped presents
Crayons
Playskool Toolkit
Tickle Me Elmo

# SOUND EFFECTS

Elmo laugh and tickle noises

# THE PERSEVERATORS
## (Inspired by the works of Molière)

## CHARACTERS

GUILLAUME: A French nobleman

HUGO: Another French nobleman

MICHELLE: An IKEA employee

## SETTING

An IKEA café

# THE PERSEVERATORS

*Guillaume and Hugo are sitting in an IKEA café, enjoying a meal.*

GUILLAUME.
> Jove! Such meaty orbs, such viscous gravy
> Abed mashed potatoes, heavens save me!
> My friend, have you ever eaten so fine
> Real Swedish cuisine for five-ninety-nine!

HUGO.
> And don't forget the lingonberry sauce…

GUILLAUME.
> How could I?! Quite frankly, I'm at a loss.
> To find the words for this alien fruit.
> But whether red or mauve, its stem hirsute,
> This mystic berry can't fail to impress.

HUGO.
> THE IKEA EXPERIENCE!

GUILLAUME.
>                       Bon c'est!

HUGO.
> Oh, resplendent, navigable café!
> Breathe in the tact and then pick up your tray.

GUILLAUME.
> Many options for you to pick and choose,
> Impossible for you to get the blues.
> Sumptuous Swedish sweets, that can't be bad:
> Vanilla Cake and Tårta Mörk Choklad.
> The latter is a treat that is quite nice,
> Almond pie with a drizzle made from rice.
> They sit so neatly in their plastic case.

HUGO.
>The double doors reflect your smiling face!
>Chicken fingers are present to entice.
>Those or meatballs? May have to roll the dice!
>Make your choice, and speak clearly to Michelle,
>"Please stir that gravy, it's starting to gel!"
>Sophistication here is far from lore,
>The soups always differ from jour to jour!
>And nothing perks the minds of two bright gents,
>Like cups of coffee for sev'nty-five cents.

GUILLAUME.
>Caffeine's a must to start us on this ride.
>Save room for hot dogs on the other side.
>The cinnamon rolls also can't be missed,
>So have another cup, please, I insist.
>A hundred thanks I owe you, mon ami,
>An arm and leg a mover's cost would be.

HUGO.
>No worries friend, I have this store down pat.
>You will need much help furnishing your flat.
>For now, we'll chat about your new bedroom.
>You'll want new pieces, I have to assume.
>A piece that would suggest a bach'lor's life
>With no sign of children, no sign of wife.
>The perfect choice would be the Hemnes set
>To pair with a post-coital cigarette.

GUILLAUME.
>Now, now, friend we've gone over this before
>And the pre-set sets are nice but…

HUGO.
>                                    You boor!
>Just follow the gray concrete path today,
>And see the genius of IKEA's way.
>The Hemnes set comes completely complete!
>And this functional wonder's no small feat.
>A full-sized box-spring; two pillows, two throws;
>The spread: white with black, little squiggly bows.
>The dresser drawers are strong and built quite wide,
>They open and close with a healthy glide.
>Far right, a vanity hutch by Grundvok

And beside that: The Yünd grandfather clock,
Majestic, imposing, and finely tuned,
Inspired by Hemnes' grandfather Yünd.
And women are without defense, my dear.
Who'd jilt a stylist/scholar/financier?!

GUILLAUME.

Hemnes knows his craft, no argument here,
But he's not a designer without peer.
I've often pictured my vanity hutch,
With a mirror from Mongstad and a touch…

HUGO.

That room wouldn't work aesthetically!
Textures mixed uncopacetically!
You have misread the designer's vision
Which influences ev'ry decision.
Here, the designers fit in sep'rate grooves,
Disregard this and disparage their oeuvres.
Think on the Sofielund walnut effect—

GUILLAUME.

My friend, you've always been so circumspect!

HUGO.

I know you disagree but hear me out.
A classy place bestows on you much clout.
Brokhult cabinets hold both forks and wine;
The natural light gleams on ev'ry tine.
They give you this structure for a reason.
Your insult is nothing short of treason.
You can't just mix and match IKEA sets.
Gorm plus Malms equals one odd kitchenette.
It's just that your idea would never flow,
IKEA fixed this problem long ago.

GUILLAUME.

I've listened to you on your insistence,
But you don't comprehend my resistance.
I, myself, am able to pick and choose
And not be constrained by their narrow views
I'm going to take my black Tvörk table—
Because I'm freethinking and am able—
And put it in my Hemnes themèd room
Though it might give IKEA cause to fume.

I'll take the Vidstrup or Randerup rug
And then—oh, don't drop that stackable mug!
I do declare right now for all to hear
Throughout this winding maze and I'll be clear!
I'll buy a dresser, counter, and drawer,
But I will not be an IKEA whore.

HUGO.

Your point of view has soured my good mood,
Your comments were so loud and awf'lly crude.
I understand, you weren't very subtle,
Allow me to offer a rebuttal.
This company believes in what it sells
They care for all monsieurs and mademoiselles.
Your dream to top IKEA is futile.
It is less futuristic than feudal.
IKEA's prices often do impress,
You didn't come today under duress.
You think you're stylish? Your poverty's clear:
You want champagne, but can barely buy beer.
Your thinking's off, you're clearly not awake
To shun furniture stores that sell you cake.

GUILLAUME.

My stance is firm, I will not compromise,
And neither will you is what I surmise.
Call off this fight, I'll say it was a draw.
You can't understand this je ne sais quoi.
I will not play into their master-plan
Big-business stuff: I'm really not a fan.
Unless you quit your rude shenanigans
I'll leave and find Raymour and Flanigan's!

HUGO.

I can't believe you'd bring up R and F!
Hearing those names makes me want to go deaf!
This "je ne sais quoi" stuff is quite an act,
You are clearly just a je ne sais quack!

GUILLAUME.

It's just like you to say something like that
You're such a busybody and a brat!

HUGO.

I will exact revenge—you no-good wench!

GUILLAUME.
>What will you use? A tiny Allen wrench?

HUGO.
>And now that's it, that is the final straw.
>Stop talking now! Just shut your goddamn maw!
>Avast! I'll be convicted of arson!
>I'll torch those books of yours by Stieg Larsson.

GUILLAUME.
>I like those books! Too bad there are no more.

HUGO.
>I know, so sad. They said there would be four.

GUILLAUME.
>If you could just see this place through MY eyes,
>You would see there is so much to despise.

HUGO.
>And if you had any visual sense,
>You'd understand just why you sound so DENSE.

>*Enter Michelle.*

MICHELLE.
>Excuse me please, don't mean to interrupt,
>I hear complaints are starting to erupt.
>So finish up your food and clear your tray.
>We want to serve more than two guys today.

GUILLAUME.
>My good man, we're finishing up a chat…

MICHELLE.
>Sir, I think I can lend a hand with that.
>I overheard what you both had to say.
>I'd like the chance to weigh in, if I may:

>*To Hugo:*

>You scolded him for not buying a set?
>Questionable reason for you to fret…

>*To Guillaume:*

>And you criticized his favorite shop
>Went on and on and on and wouldn't stop!
>The two of you don't seem to realize
>That secretly both of you are allies.
>IKEA's trick is ecumenical.

Everything here is quite identical.
All this goes with that, and all that with this;
All who think diff'rent are sadly remiss.
So there it is, the both of you are wrong.
Now suck it up and eat and move along.
A softer tone you'll take—I am adamant,
Or I will have to call in management.

*Exit Michelle.*

HUGO.
Who knew Michelle was great at mediation?
GUILLAUME.
Ev'ryone's staring… let's go… let's hasten.

## End of Play

# PROPERTY LIST

Plates of food
Mugs of coffee

# PEANUTS &
# CRACKER JACK
## (Inspired by the works of Neil Simon)

# CHARACTERS

AIDAN

GLORIA

CAROL

# SETTING

High in the stands of Progressive Field,
home of the Cleveland Indians.

# PEANUTS &
# CRACKER JACK

*Aidan and Gloria at a Cleveland Indians baseball game. They sit way up in the stands. Their body language suggests they are well acquainted with each other, though their relationship has seen better days.*

AIDAN. How does one become an umpire? Do you need special accreditation? A license or certificate or something? At what point does someone say, "Mommy, I'm gonna be an umpire?" I can't imagine what that would sound like to a parent: "Oh, that's great, honey? An umpire—a fine, noble profession. Of course we'd have preferred you to become an actual judge, or an actual baseball player but an umpire will do just fine."

GLORIA. Dad used to ump my brother's games. The other dads hated him. We all had to run to the car after the games to avoid the wrath and fury.

AIDAN. Somehow I think your dad and his five sons could have taken a few unruly, beer-bellied, pride-in-my-boy fathers.

GLORIA. We had a few good scraps. One time Mr. Mulligan and his sons got into it with us. I scratched Bobby Mulligan's cornea and nearly ripped out one of Shelly Mulligan's pigtails before we leapt into the trunk of our station wagon and careened out of the parking lot.

AIDAN. ... But did your dad have to be certified or anything to be the ump?

GLORIA. No... Weren't you on the baseball team in high school?

AIDAN. Yeah—sorta. I was the ball-shine guy.

GLORIA. Ball-shine guy?

AIDAN. Yeah, you know, the guy who's got the towel and the spray and makes sure the balls are shiny for the... you didn't have those?

GLORIA.  Nope… Four years as the ball shine guy?

AIDAN.  Not quite, I lasted two years in the great American pas-time. However, I did go on to achieve success in mock trial/moot court and school plays. First King Lear with acne. The beard didn't even cover it all. It's a good game, huh?

GLORIA.  Oh, yeah! Great game. Lots of action! Only the fifth inning and we've already put up six runs. The other guys can barely get a hit in.

*Beat.*

AIDAN.  Jeez, the ball is so small…

GLORIA.  Yeah—we're in the rafters. The more you pay the bigger the ball gets.

AIDAN.  I know—but… you can't even see it. Whenever anyone gets passed the ball it looks like they're catching fireflies—That guy just did a fouetté.

GLORIA.  Can we just enjoy the day?

AIDAN.  Gloria, if I didn't win these tickets from DJ Davey's Daily Giveaway you'd be spending the afternoon diagnosing other people's dogs at the dog park. Without hand sanitizer.

GLORIA.  You date a vet, that's what you get.

> *Beat. A voice from the crowd shouts, "I've seen porches with better swings!"*

This is my first time going to a Cleveland game… We were Tigers fans through and through. My father would kill me if he knew I went to an Indians game.

AIDAN.  Are they even still allowed to be called the Indians? I thought we had abandoned that label.

GLORIA.  Look, Aidan, if you had such a moral opposition to the name, we shouldn't have come.

AIDAN.  I just feel as though we, as a collective society, had banded together against that term. You never see teams like the Georgetown Gringos or the Kansas City Honkies. It's just the Indians or the Braves. Or the Redskins! It's always the Native Americans! In fact, I'm not even sure the right term is "Native American." "Indigenous"? I'm not really sure. What does that say about me? See, I'm part of the problem too!

GLORIA.  Yeah, and you buy Land O'Lakes butter by the tub!

AIDAN.  I'm gonna do a piece about this for *The Stickler*.

GLORIA.  How's readership for *The Stickler*?

AIDAN. Not this again…

GLORIA. No, I'm really asking. I'm interested in your writing pursuits. I know it means a lot to you.

AIDAN. You're doing that thing again where you belittle my profession. Perhaps readership is low these days, but you forget, one needs to build a portfolio. I just need to continue posting articles so that agents can see I'm ever writing.

GLORIA. Yes, I understand that, but maybe it would be helpful to write for somewhere other than your own personal blog—

AIDAN. *(Correcting her.)* —Scholarly web-based publication.

GLORIA. Sure… maybe you should write for *someone else* is what I'm saying.

AIDAN. You don't understand, Gloria. You don't understand and you NEVER have! I have 130 subscribers. That's not nothing.

GLORIA. And 110 of them are in Barrow, Alaska.

AIDAN. That's the whole town!

GLORIA. Yeah! Because it never gets dark there! They're desperate for sleep!

> Enter Carol, the ballpark merchandise salesperson. She is dressed up in her uniform and has a hawking tray hanging from her neck. She is disgruntled and unhappy and makes no effort to hide it.

CAROL. I GOT $5 HOT DOGS. GET YOUR $5 HOT DOGS—WITH TAX THEY COME OUT TO SIX AND A QUARTER. WHO'S BUYIN'? I GOT WATERS, SODAS, ICED TEA. THE GUY WHO SELLS BEERS GETS PAID FIFTY CENTS MORE THAN ME!

AIDAN. Want anything? I could call over Rosie the Riveter.

GLORIA. Sure, Aidan. We're here, aren't we… could you grab her?

CAROL. I GOT PRETZELS, PEANUTS, NACHOS, CRACK-ER JACKS—BUT THEY DON'T COME CHEAP! OH NO! GOURMET SLOP, THIS IS! THE HORSE IN THE HOT DOGS WAS FED CAVIAR BEFORE THE SLAUGHTER!

AIDAN. *(Signaling Carol.)* Hey! Yoo hoo! Excuse me!

CAROL. Ohhh, I see ya, guy! Comin' right up.

AIDAN. How are you today, miss?

CAROL. Oh, I'm a low-wage worker in a society that enables poverty and devalues women. I'm dandy. What can I get you? An $11 knish?

AIDAN. No… um… Gloria, what would you like?

GLORIA. Oh! I'll just have some funnel cake and a beer for now—
CAROL. I don't do beer—*he* does beer and *he'll* be down as soon as he's finished flirting with the test-your-pitch girl.
GLORIA. Yeah—okay, no problem…
CAROL. Anything else?
AIDAN. Yeah—I'd like something quintessentially baseball-y… What ya got?
CAROL. Uh, steroids?
AIDAN. I'll just take a bag of peanuts.
CAROL. Small, medium, large or Bonkers?
AIDAN. Um… small?
CAROL. That comes to an even $15.

     *Gloria goes into her purse for her wallet.*

AIDAN. You gotta be kidding me!
CAROL. No buddy—I am not kidding you. Did the math myself. But you can do it, sir. You can be the first guy to watch a baseball game without eating the food here! You can do it. Don't be a sucker!
GLORIA. When in Rome, right?

     *She forks over the $15.*

CAROL. Suit yourself. The social security pool will be bankrupt by the time you could retire anyway. Retirement is a carrot dangled in front of the proletariat by the one percent.

     *She gathers their snacks and passes them down to Aidan and Gloria.*

AIDAN. Thanks…
CAROL. *(Sarcastic.)* You're welcome!

     *She starts to exit.*

AIDAN. Yeesh, what a charmer.
CAROL. $5 HOT DOGS! GET YER $5 HOT DOGS. GET THEM WHILE THEY'RE HOT AND BALMY IN THIS DAY-OLD WATER!

     *Exits.*

GLORIA. It's really not about the game is it?
AIDAN. What do you mean?
GLORIA. Look around you: Only ten percent of what you're looking at is baseball game, the other ninety percent are ads for… like… insurance. Or office supplies. At least I need Scotch tape,

*(Calling out.)* I'm all set with insurance, thank you! It's so corporate! What's the point of coming to a baseball game?

AIDAN. To see the kind of people who never come to the library?

GLORIA. To see superhumans do superhuman things! The slowest guy here runs faster than the fastest guy in your high school. They're getting missiles thrown at their heads, and they're supposed to swing at them. It's amazing!

AIDAN. But all you do is sit on your rear end and watch it, 'cause you can't participate. All you can do to participate is sit and eat and buy things and absorb. That's why they've basically painted the place with ads. They've got your number and they suck you dry like a whale slurping down krill. Hey, not a bad title for a *Stickler* piece...

GLORIA. Makes me miss watching the high school games...

> *An organ is heard over the loudspeaker playing the "Charge!" chant. Folks in the stands chant along. Gloria and Aidan do not.*

Look Aidan, there's something I want to talk to you about.

AIDAN. Well, this seems like the perfect time, since I have no idea what's happening in this game.

GLORIA. You are so on edge lately! I don't know if it's *The Stickler*, or if things are especially hectic at the library these days—

> *He gives her a look.*

—but it's been hard being with you when you're this tense. I feel like I'm sleeping next to a two-by-four.

AIDAN. Well, I'm sorry, Gloria. I'm sorry that my work doesn't have me singing songs at the end of the day. Maybe at the animal clinic you get stressed over some especially cuddly kittens.

GLORIA. You're always doing this! You're always reducing my doctorate to... doggie daycare!

> *Beat.*

There's an open position at the Cincinnati *Tribune*. I think it would be great for you. A copy editing position.

AIDAN. Oh god! A copy editor. How lower-level can you get—

GLORIA. It's called "entry" level, because unless you're already "in" the industry, you need to enter it... Look, you're more than qualified and you'd be great at it. And you'd be able to meet some of the editors at the paper. You could keep writing for *The Stickler* and maybe they'd eventually start publishing some of your pieces.

AIDAN. This seems very well thought out, Gloria. Do you go to work every morning and talk these things over with the impounded animals?

GLORIA. Don't be like this…

AIDAN. Not all of us can expect fulfillment in our nine-to-fives. We can't all feel like Snow White, saving the urban woodland creatures from weirdos and their garbage disposals. Cincinnati: no thanks.

GLORIA. My cousin Beth lives in Cincinnati, she could help us get on our feet. We're talking about opening our own animal shelter. This is my chance to move up, and since you aren't exactly tied down I figured…

AIDAN. You figured what? You figured what?!

*Carol reenters.*

CAROL. *(Blankly.)* Hot dogs! Hot dogs! Get yer hot dogs.

*She takes a deep breath and rolls her eyes.*

No GMOs! No hormones! Get yer all-natural, authentic ballpark franks!

GLORIA. *(To Aidan.)* Someone's been spoken to…

CAROL. How about nachos! Now made with real cheese!

AIDAN. *(To Gloria.)* I'm sick of this bull! Ballpark franks have always been a ripoff and now they think they can get away with it by calling them "all-natural." I'm going to write all about this in *The Stickler.*

GLORIA. Give it a rest Aidan, you're not gonna win a Pulitzer for hot dogs.

AIDAN. *(Standing, at Carol.)* I call bull, miss!

CAROL. *(Nonplussed.)* You rang, sir?

AIDAN. I call *bull.* How much they charging for all that organic? You going to tell me that organic hot dog is worth $5.

CAROL. Sir, I am telling you that. I'm telling you that because they gave me a box of hot dogs, attached it to a cash register, and told me to sell it to the hot-dog eating public for $5.

GLORIA. *(Stepping in.)* You know what, I'll take a box of Cracker Jacks. Not going to spend my day penny pinching with Ebenezer Scrooge here.

AIDAN. *(To Gloria.)* You gonna do that? *(To Carol.)* And you're gonna take that? You have the audacity to take $6 of her hard-earned money for a box of Cracker Jacks? I could get those for her at CVS for a quarter of the price.

CAROL. Then go eat at a pharmacy, sir, that's what things cost here.

AIDAN. You ought to be ashamed!

CAROL. *(Quickly losing her cool.)* I ought to be ashamed? You're at a baseball game in a tweed jacket… and loafers! You think I LIKE selling this overpriced trash? Need a napkin? Just wipe your face with my MBA. This whole city has.

AIDAN. Be that as it may, you're part of the problem!

CAROL. And what is it you do, Atticus Finch?

AIDAN. I'm a writer. I publish a scholarly web-based publication in which I write longform articles on social justice and reform.

GLORIA. *(To Carol.)* He works six shifts a week at the reference desk of the library.

CAROL. And the truth comes out! Everyone knows these hot dogs are FILTH! AND that they cost way too much. Doesn't take an investigative journalist to figure that out. But any idea what it's like to balance a huge tray high up on a concrete staircase?

AIDAN. You coulda worked at a public pool and sold reasonably priced snacks at a normal altitude!

CAROL. And if you could actually string together a sentence you might be published by *Mother Jones* instead of your bogus blog. I don't see Katie Couric yelling at a hot dog lady in the middle of Progressive Field! Oh, and if you hear from any "public pools" I'll be writing a cover letter on the fryolator. HOT DOGS!

> *She storms off.*

AIDAN. Where does she get off?!

GLORIA. Where do you get off?! We won these tickets and we were just supposed to come and have some fun together which we never really do anymore anyway. All you did was berate me and embarrass me. I only want you to succeed and I've only ever encouraged you, even if the AARP monthly pamphlet has a more alert readership than *The Stickler.* I'm going home. And I'm going to Cincinnati. I'm sorry.

> *She turns to leave. As she exits we hear a CRACK! An offstage voice yells, "Fly ball!" Gloria turns back around. There is excited murmuring throughout the crowd. Aidan, feeling dejected, looks up for just a moment. His eyes widen and he reaches for the sky. The murmuring builds as Aidan catches the fly ball. Another offstage voice shouts, "Way to go, guy!" The crowd goes wild. Yet another voice shouts, "You're on the jumbotron!" Aidan turns to face the jumbotron. He takes in*

*the joy of this moment. Gloria makes to leave again. The cheering begins to die and just before it dissipates totally:*

AIDAN. *(To Gloria.)* Wait!

*She turns back to him.*

Gloria. This can't be how it ends. At a baseball game? A free baseball game? I don't even like baseball. And I don't know what the hell it was that made me so completely ornery tonight, or last night, or every night for as long as we can remember. Maybe I'm more sensitive than I want to admit. Maybe my stupid pride is easier to live with than the fact that no one but a bunch of zombified insomniacs read my blog. Yes—It's a blog. No one has ever said "scholarly web-based publication." It's a wonder and a gift you've never called me out on that. Look—I proclaim to know a lot about social justice, maybe I don't know anything at all—but it would be a social *in*justice for me to let you just walk out of here. Not only because you drove, but because I love you more than anything in this world—and definitely more than anything in Cleveland. If you'll have me, I'll apply to that job in Cincinnati tonight. If you won't... I'll understand... but at least take this ball I caught. To remember our first Indians game.

GLORIA. Does it make you mad that I think everything you just said is more convincing than anything you've ever written for *The Stickler*?

AIDAN. A little embarrassed perhaps... but no.

*Gloria returns to Aidan. He hands her the ball. They sit down.*

GLORIA. We shouldn't waste free tickets...

*They watch the game for a moment, munching on their snacks. After a moment, they take hands. A moment later they simultaneously offer each other:*

AIDAN. Peanut?                    GLORIA. Cracker Jack?

## End of Play

# PROPERTY LIST

Hawking Tray
Peanuts
Box of Cracker Jack
Cash
Baseball

# SOUND EFFECTS

Organ playing "Charge!" chant
Cheers and voices from the crowd

# UPRIGHT & LOCKED
## (Inspired by the works of Samuel Beckett)

# CHARACTERS

WOMAN

VOICE FROM ABOVE

# SETTING

An airplane.

# UPRIGHT & LOCKED

*Pitch black.*

*Lights snap on to reveal two pairs of large garbage cans with an aisle-sized space in between. One can has a Woman inside. Her head and shoulders are visible. The can is mostly shiny but beginning to tarnish in spots. On the can somewhere is a sticker that reads: 221 D*

*The other cans are similarly labeled. The stickers are beginning to fade. On the floor next to the garbage cans are the lids.*

*Now back to Woman. She is an ordinary, miserable-looking middle-aged woman. Not miserable in the sense that catastrophe or tragedy have struck, but miserable in the ordinary, "Why do things that should be simple have to be so miserable?" way.*

*She wears a decent, simple dress, though we will never see the bottom of it. Her hair is neatly done.*

*She is sleeping uncomfortably but soundly.*

*A recorded message comes over the intercom.*

*The voice sounds relentlessly cheery. Yet, sad.*

VOICE FROM ABOVE. Thanks for flying with United Airlines. We hope you enjoyed your flight. Please wait for the passengers in the rows before you to gather their belongings and exit before leaving your seat. We hope you enjoy your stay in Shreveport. A flight attendant should be by to collect your garbage… *(With scorn.)* Your refuse… Your filth.

*During this recording, Woman snorts herself awake. She starts to gather her "belongings," crumpled magazines and garbage from many, many inflight meals. But when she realizes no one is coming to collect it any time soon, she lets it all drop back in and around the can.*

For those continuing on to Cheyenne, Fresno, and Montgomery please remain in your seats and keep the aisles clear.

*Woman pauses in consternation for a while. She remembers her journey isn't over. She sinks.*

We're committed to making your flight safe and comfortable. So before we depart, please pay attention to this brief safety demonstration. This information can help you if there's an emergency, so please pay close attention…
Otherwise you might miss him altogether…

*This last sentence strikes the woman as peculiar.*

If you are in First, Premium Business Comfort, Business Comfort, Business, or Comfort classes, please pay attention to the friendly, attractive flight attendant in front of you. If you are in Economy or Economy Steerage, please listen up.

*The Woman reacts and looks bemused.*

All carry on items should now be stored securely and all aisles, exits and bulkhead areas should be clear.
Don't worry, you'll arrive at your final destination to catch him before the end of his shift.

*Woman looks up, slightly surprised, then looks down sadly.*

Your mobile phones and all other electronic devices should be turned off. Once airborne, we'll let you know when you can use approved electronic devices. You will find a list of approved electronic devices in the safety brochure tucked into the pouch in front of you. You will also find *Skymall* magazine—a premiere guide to purchase some of the finest products you can find in the sky.

*Woman pulls a phonebook-sized* Skymall *catalogue out of the can. She looks at it, considers it, and, upon realizing she won't actually purchase anything, launches it into the wings.*

As you leave the gate make sure your seatbelt is fastened.

*The* Skymall *is launched back at her. She resignedly puts it in the can.*

To fasten, insert the metal tip into the buckle and adjust the strap so it's low and tight across your lap. Adjust the metal tip so it's low and tight across the fastener. Adjust the fastener so it's tucked securely beneath your belly.

*She doesn't follow.*

To release the belt, just lift the top of the buckle. Please remain seated with your seatbelt fastened every time the seatbelt sign is on. Even if the sign is off, you should keep the seatbelt fastened.

> *As we hear this, Woman, with great difficulty, manages to fasten her seatbelt inside the can. We hear the clattering of the buckle against the side of the can as she struggles.*

There's a strong possibility he might recognize you.

> *Startled, Woman looks around the stage for someone or something else who's hearing what she's hearing.*

Smoking is not allowed *(Spoken condescendingly.)* on any Delta flight and federal law prohibits tampering with, disabling, or destroying a restroom smoke detector.

He might still sleep with the teddy bear you left him. It could sit against his pillow waiting for him to come to bed. He might lie nightly holding the bear close to his heart and thinking of who you might be.

Or... maybe not.

> *The Woman is distressed and perplexed, on the verge of tearing her hair out.*

A flight attendant will be coming around with headphones, pillows, and neck rests for purchase. We will also be offering alcoholic beverages, soda, water, and chips for purchase. Complimentary peanuts will be provided at no charge.

> *A bag of peanuts is hurled at her from the wings.*

If you are traveling with your canine companion this afternoon and purchased the Aer Lingus Pet Comfort package, your pet will be receiving their fifth and final meal of the flight once we reach our cruising altitude.

> *We hear a muffled bark or squeak from deep within Woman's can. It is not necessarily a dog.*

There are six exits on this plane: four doors, two on each side, and two window exits over the wings. Two trap doors beneath the wings and a secret passage from the first-class lavatory. Each door has a detachable slide that can be used for floatation… or fun!

For those passengers who opted for the "Safety First" flight package, life vests and oxygen packets can be found in the pouch in front of you. For those who did not, please be especially sure to fill out your next-of-kin form also in the pouch in front of you.

*Woman goes to look and then remembers she did not purchase the "Safety First" flight package. Takes a plastic bag from her can, swings it to fill with air, and ties it shut. She puts the bag in the can.*

All exits are clearly marked with an exit sign. However, if there is a loss of power and cabin visibility is reduced, red lights along the aisles will guide you to the nearest exit. Please remember we will evacuate the plane beginning with the passengers seated at the front of the aircraft. For those of you in Economy Steerage—keep track of your lid—it may help you keep your head above water… but only literally.

*The Woman reaches to pull the lid a little closer but she can't quite reach it. She gives up.*

There's also a possibility he'll want to stay with the people who raised him.

*Woman is in agony.*

Now before we take off be sure your seat is upright and locked, your tray table is put away, and all carry-on items are properly stowed. For our passengers in First, Premium Business Comfort, Business Comfort, Business, or Comfort classes, or JetBlue Extra Legroom seating, the flight duration should be about six hours, twelve minutes. For those passengers flying in Economy or Economy Steerage, it may take a little longer. Thanks for your attention.

*The plane has been moving. We hear the sounds of it taking off again.*

A brief announcement for those passengers continuing on this plane from Caribou to Amarillo: There will be a delay. Thank you!

*Woman stares out.*

*Restless, Woman reaches into the can and pulls out a novel— it should be a very popular, recognizable title. She tries to open it and read but she can't find a comfortable position. She puts the book away. She reaches below again and pulls up a small pillow and blanket issued to her by the airline. She opens up the blanket and finds a position where she is semi-covered by the blanket and leaning on the pillow. She looks miserable.*

I'd now like to introduce our inflight entertainment selection: *The Sound of Music.*

*The woman is surprised by a light shining in her face from inside the can. Simultaneously music begins to play. It is obnoxiously gleeful, but also distorted and odd as it echoes throughout the can. The music slowly grows louder and louder until it fills the theater. The Woman is desperate.*

*Blackout.*

## End of Play

# PROPERTY LIST

Crumpled magazines and garbage
Phonebook-sized *Skymall*
Bag of peanuts
Plastic bag
Novel
Small pillow and blanket

# SOUND EFFECTS

Clattering of seatbelt buckle against can
Muffled bark or squeak of an animal
Plane taking off
Obnoxiously gleeful music

# THE MOST LAMENTABLE COMEDIE OF MOIRA AND ROSA

(Inspired by the works
of William Shakespeare)

## CHARACTERS

MOIRA: Mother of two.

ROSA: Mother of two.

GREG: Father of none.

## SETTING

The manager's office of the Amazon.com warehouse.

# THE MOST LAMENTABLE COMEDIE OF MOIRA AND ROSA

*Robbinsville, NJ. Manager's office of an Amazon.com warehouse. Moira and Rosa are seated.*

GREG.  Pilferers! Rogues! Base cowards! I'll none of it! Thou'st gorged thyselves on the fruits and meats of thine noble trade. Thou has advantage took of a gen'rous thirty percent employee discount. You have picked more than you have packed *(Points to pile of boxes.)*, and now you are caught! Didst thou not think of the customers, their precious merchandise suddenly made "NOT IN STOCK" by your tomfoolery?! As for my part, I will see you erased from the History of Amazon. Once I'm done washing your smudge from our ledgers, no one but your families shall know of your bad deeds or your good deeds… if there be any. Stay you here whilst I seek out my superior. He'll no doubt bid thee resign and say, "Anon, 'til we meet again in court."

    *Exit Greg.*

ROSA.  Alack-a-day, Moira. Too far we rose,
    And like ignoble Icarus we fall.
    Shame and lamentation are our badges.
    Oh! Our families! Our reputations!
MOIRA.  Amazon.com was absolute bliss.
    A palace where all products of all brands
    Are cheap and eas'ly attained by any.
ROSA.  Not only are we banished from paradise,
    Our bank accounts are stunted in their growth;
    Upon Christmas Day, my children shall mew:
    "Our stockings are thinnéd—what gives, Mother?"

And I'll cry, "Santa took too much crap last year,
And so Santa's no crap to give today."
MOIRA. But thinkst why we stole, Rosa! Remember thine
  Children. Cute, yes, but expensive, and so needy!
  Gah! *I* too am assailed with adolescence!
  Bake sales, museum trips, soccer matches, zounds!
  Bar and Bat Mitzvah season is nigh, then
  Sickly-Sweet Sixteens with foul, prating sluts.
ROSA. And sleepovers! I'm a damned innkeeper!
  One must take some for themselves to keep up,
  'Specially at minimum wage, no doubt.
  Alas, we are dead to Amazon now.

  *Rosa cries.*

MOIRA. And yet, we stole these wares to serve a cause.
  A *greater* cause. Worth the toil and trouble.
  For once the stuff was took, we reviewed it.
  Published our reviews in verse, or in prose.
  We spent more time writing than stealing.
ROSA. We made a pact to help ignorant minds!
  Abscond with stuff and set down our reviews;
  Try every trifle here at Amazon,
  And with two stars or five their fate is writ.
MOIRA. We're heroines of the common man,
  For what's took is replaced with sound advice.
  Ev'ry product was researched and tested
  And with good judgement, starred for the masses
  You Rosa, who did speak nary a peep
  Before our escapades, let forth a gush
  Of poetry and prose…
ROSA.                        Like a geyser
MOIRA. Uh-huh, remember your earliest verse:
  "The Duck Dynasty Youth Archery Set:
  A healthy tool, I thought, for teenage angst.
  How wrong I was—the squirrels can speak to that.
  Now I'm raising a budding psychopath."
ROSA. My words were more cute than were substantial,
  Though my thoughts were steadfast and arrow-like.
  Treat all consumers like we would our kids;
  Bestow respect and class upon the web;
  Too often is the platform abuséd,

Hackneyed missives from countless two-bit frauds.

MOIRA.  Rosa, if we are mark'd for fire—now
　　Is the time we must act, and act we shall.
　　Thinkst on yesterday's batch of stuff you stole
　　And type ere our opinions slip away.

ROSA.  You hearten me, okay let's do the deed,
　　I'll start us off with this lofty quatrain:
　　"Campbell's Chunky Chicken Soup was applauded,
　　Its savory goodness could not be beat;
　　But opening the can is to be frauded
　　With fingernail-sized hunks of myst'ry meat."
　　Now you—and remember'st how slow I type.

MOIRA.  "Oh, Roku 2, Roku 2
　　What is a Netflix worth, if not for you?
　　Reliable streaming all night through
　　Oh Roku 2, Roku 2."

ROSA.  My God, you seize my heart with syllables

MOIRA.  Here's one! Godiva Assorted Truffles:
　　"Ate from a box with twenty-four pieces,
　　Plan'd to devour alone in the tub;
　　Opened to find all melted and sloppy;
　　Choc'late in my bubbles and down the drain!
　　In the state of Belgium, something's rotten."

ROSA.  Five stars for the Rain-X window repair kit

MOIRA.  But soft, what rock through yonder windshield breaks?

ROSA.  Flowable silicone: sticky as sap
　　What else? Oh… seals up the cracks in a flash!

MOIRA.  Posted! Now type my next analysis.
　　A product used quite often in my home:
　　Your simple, quintessential ballpoint pen.
　　Accidentally snatched Z-grips 'stead of Bic:
　　Clicks too feeble to retract the point!
　　Made my pockets look like a Rorschach test.

ROSA.  Ugh! Out, out damned splotch!

MOIRA.  A pen with an infrastructure so weak
　　Brings out my rage—had to steal more Tide!

ROSA.  If you click us, do we not…

MOIRA.　　　　　　　　　　Bleed and bleed
　　And bleed everywhere and on everything
　　One star and one-way trip to the trash.

ROSA. I always admired your terse adjudications.
   All this is well-penned. Witful, more substance,
   Less prose. Online reviews are lit'rature.
MOIRA. And it makes for less trips to the store
ROSA. I have told thee often and I re-tell thee again and again:
   I Hate… the store. Quick, another ere Greg…

*Pause.*

Moira, it's no use, no use. We're deceived
By ourselves! Amazon holds these reviews,
Clutched in their wire hands. They'll no doubt kill,
And hide our words, once they know the authors.
You heard Greg's threats! Like a droopy-eared hound,
He'll sniff out these reviews, and once we're smelled,
They will be from the web untimely ripp'd.

*Pause.*

MOIRA. Rosa, friend, typed words are scribbles in sand,
   'Tis true, but the fonts and stars of our art
   Matter not. Thinkst of where our reviews live:
   In teens with Paypal accounts, moms with Prime,
   Dads who have forgotten their kids' birthdays,
   All now have frame of ref'rence when they shop.
ROSA. Does it matter, if they'll be eraséd?
MOIRA. One controls so little. Our posts will die,
   But they can't kill our valued expertise
   Or change the minds of folks whose minds we've chang'd.
   We'll take our punishment tactfully, and,
   As honest maids, die a' peace—money saved.
ROSA. Your words hath made the world a glass window
   So clear that pigeons might soar into it.
   All the world's a webpage—
MOIRA.                 Thou understands!
ROSA. And every webpage has its webmaster,
   And in their time delete many good posts.
   My kids shall hear of mine Robin Hood deeds,
   Whilst I hold them tightly abreast as mothers do,
   And bid them go and hide the stuff I stole.

*Enter Greg with piece of paper.*

GREG. Hear me. Chad, my supervisor and mentor alike, has re-titled you deceitful knaves Co-Chiefs of Online Marketing. Ere the ink was dry on your pink slips, and I had lifted them up guillotine-like to lop off your lying heads, Chad discovered your "magnificent" reviews. Apparently your reviews are the loftiest poetic nuggets he's ever seen, and whatever way the winds of Chad blow, I sway with them. *(He smiles.)* Now, rise and follow me to your new station. Come! Give me your hands, if we be friends, and Sir Chad shall restore amends.

*Exeunt.*

## End of Play

# PROPERTY LIST

Computer

# THE EL TAQUERIA
## (Inspired by the works
## of Anton Chekhov)

# CHARACTERS

LORELAILITA: Eldest sister

SHANNONSUELA: Middle sister

AMANDITA: Youngest sister

ARMANDO: The brother

TÍO COCINERO: The uncle

# SETTING

A Taco Bell in North Adams, MA.

# THE EL TAQUERIA

*A seemingly normal afternoon at a seemingly normal Taco Bell in North Adams, MA. It is the spring. Faintly from outside we hear the on and off whirring of a bulldozer—but we don't think much of it. Amandita, the youngest sister, is slowly cutting coupons out of a newspaper. Shannonsuela, the middle sister, is rushing about.*

AMANDITA. Business has never been this slow. Not since Father died. How long has it been since we've had a customer? My goodness, you'd think the middle school ran out of weed! There's really nothing to do: We've cleaned the tables, the grills, changed the roach traps…

SHANNONSUELA. Don't worry. It's just that post-fourth-meal, pre-breakfast slump. People will be arriving any minute. I'm so glad the place looks great for Armando's arrival.

AMANDITA. Oh, that's right! I forgot Armando was coming today. Gosh, I barely remember him. It's been so long.

SHANNONSUELA. It has been. He hasn't been back since he went off to law school.

AMANDITA. God, I'll always remember that day Armando got on that Peter Pan bus to law school. The sun was shining behind all those clouds. He left us each with a little present. What did he give you, Shannonsuela?

SHANNONSUELA. An egg timer.

AMANDITA. He gave me a travel thesaurus. I'll never understand why…

SHANNONSUELA. Listen, if anyone will know what to do it's him. We may even get to put up one of those "Grand Re-Opening" signs!

AMANDITA. I guess you're right. I dunno… Arlo keeps talking about a bowling alley in Pittsfield. He and I should rent the little luncheonette and make it our own. Sometimes I feel like I've taken all I can from North Adams. There's so much more to Massachusetts. I think I need a great, glittering metropolis... like Pittsfield.

SHANNONSUELA. Let's see what Armando has to say about the business when he arrives. I have the feeling once he's here we're going to be so busy we'll need you full-time on registers. But let's see—then we can talk about cafeterias in Pittsfield.

AMANDITA. Luncheonette!

SHANNONSUELA. Luncheonette, whatever. Personally, I doubt you'd even want to make a move to Pittsfield.

AMANDITA. What?! Why would you say that? All of my dreams are in Pittsfield!

SHANNONSUELA. Then why haven't you visited it? It's like a half-hour away.

AMANDITA. The fear of traffic and car sickness engulf me with inaction. But I know when the time comes, I'll kiss Arlo and kiss this town goodbye as we fly in his Ford Taurus to Pittsfield.

*Enter Lorelailita, the eldest sister. She is a trash-chic kinda girl (whatever that means to you). Dressed to the nines.*

LORELAILITA. Hiya lovebuns! How you do?! Oh I'm fabuloso! Brodie just finished his last infomercial for the Pocket Masseuse. After the success of the Summertime Yuletide Log—consumers around the world are awaiting his next invention.

*She pulls out her smartphone.*

Well, here it is! The Pocket Masseuse.

SHANNONSUELA. You mean a phone?

LORELAILITA. A wha? Oh it's a phone! HAHAHAHA—you're so funny Shannonsuela. Isn't she the kookiest, Amandita?! The Pocket Masseuse allows you unlimited access to your phone's vibration feature. You can get a massage anywhere you are!

AMANDITA. Wow! I should download it for Arlo!

*She goes to download it on her iPhone.*

LORELAILITA. You bet! Anything you want, love. Anyway—as much as I'd love to chat—Brodie and I are having about eleventy-billion investors over for a little pre-release party. So I'm going to need you to put together an order for me. Let's see—how about we do a few platters of Crunchy Taco Supremes—sour cream on the side—a few of the Cheesy Potato burritos—Let's get twenty-six

Nachos BellGrandes—a large tub of Pintos 'n' Cheese, and about fifty caramel apple empanadas. Can you do it for tomorrow, cinnabun?

AMANDITA. Hey Shannonsuela—press this up against my back!

SHANNONSUELA. Lorelailita—you can't keep coming here ordering and eating and not paying. We can't afford this… But this one last time I'll let it slide since Armando is coming home today to get us back on track!

LORELAILITA. Armando's coming back!? Oh how wonderful. Let's make the party a double feature. We'll celebrate Armando's return and Brodie's app.

AMANDITA. That's a great idea! I'll invite Arlo!

LORELAILITA. Oh my goodness—when are you two just going to tie the knot?!

AMANDITA. Lorelailita!

> *Enter Tío Cocinero, uncle to the sisters. He comes out wearing a heavily soiled apron (it looks burnt) and a chef's hat.*

TÍO COCINERO. What's all the commotion in here?! Are my beautiful nieces fighting over a man?

LORELAILITA. No! Of course not, Tío Cocinero. We were just teasing Amandita. How's it going?!

TÍO COCINERO. It's good! Lots of cooking happening here. Trying out new recipes. My latest is called the SubDonald Asado. Want to know how it's made!?

LORELAILITA. Sure!

TÍO COCINERO. Well—I go down the street to Subway and ask for a big, moist loaf of Italian Herbs and Cheese bread from Sonny. Then I go to McDonald's and pick up a few fresh McRibs. I cut one tip of the bread off and bore a deep hole into the loaf. I fill it with two McRibs, couple handfuls of cheese, some dried cilantro, and a scrambled egg. Now here's the tricky part. I take a small amount of the Quesadilla paste and fuse the bread tip back on. But there you have it—and once it's congealed, you can slice it!

LORELAILITA. Delicious! Tío—you must make a tray of those for Brodie and my soirée! We're having a huge party. Tío—you must cook. It wouldn't be the same!

TÍO COCINERO. Cook?! What purpose do I have on this soil if not to cook and nourish my people? Why, I remember my training—at the Payaso Boracho—a little Mexican-style saloon just north of here. Back then a burrito was a burrito. The size of a horse! You'd go in the back, grab a chicken, and spin it 'til its little cabeza flew right off. Ahhh, I can remember a time…

SHANNONSUELA. Okay, Tío—

AMANDITA. Hey, Tío—ever been to Pittsfield?!

SHANNONSUELA. That's enough, Amandita.

TÍO COCINERO. Lorelailita, it would be my greatest pleasure to cook for you. This family needs a celebration. Your father loved a celebration. Let me tell you—he loved having over a bunch a friends and cooking up a storm.

SHANNONSUELA. And making his daughters the waitstaff.

TÍO COCINERO. Well—

SHANNONSUELA. And leaving his family to move up north. Find his fortune creating the Straw-ber-ita and leave his daughters to salvage his little pet project.

LORELAILITA. For shame, Shannonsuela!

TÍO COCINERO. 'Twas the Straw-ber-itas that killed him!

SHANNONSUELA. Yeah! 'Cause he drank too many!

AMANDITA. Body couldn't handle all the rim salt.

LORELAILITA. Shannonsuela! Don't talk about Father that way. You know at the bottom he always cared for us.

SHANNONSUELA. Cared for us?! All our father ever cared about was Mexican-style food. We're lucky we have Armando to come and clean up his mess.

*Enter Armando. He is slightly older than the sisters and is extremely well dressed.*

AMANDITA. Armando!

SHANNONSUELA. Armando! You're back.

ARMANDO. Hello everyone. It's good to see you all.

SHANNONSUELA. Armando. Thank goodness you're here. It's been so long. We have so much to discuss.

ARMANDO. I know. And we will get to all of that, Shannonsuela. But we need to take care of the move first.

SHANNONSUELA. Move?

ARMANDO. Yes—today is moving day. Don't you see the bull-dozers?

SHANNONSUELA. Of course I see them but I thought they were here for the Dollar Barn.

ARMANDO. Dollar Barn? No—the Dollar Barn is doing great. They are here for us. You knew about this.

LORELAILITA. Knew about what?

ARMANDO. Knew about the demolition. Knew that we were in a hole deeper than what this lot is about to be. I've already done everything I can with corporate to keep this place running.

SHANNONSUELA. How were we supposed to know?

ARMANDO. From the many, many emails I've sent you over the past year.

SHANNONSUELA. I haven't been able to check work email…

ARMANDO. Why not?

TÍO COCINERO. The mouse is sticky and the keyboard is gunky!

ARMANDO. Well I don't know what to say to that—It's not something I have any control over—I was just passing on information.

SHANNONSUELA. No calls. No texts—just a postcard from Cedar Point saying, "Looking forward to seeing you at the Demo."

LORELAILITA. We thought you meant Brodie's app. And just who do you think you are! Up and leaving and coming back with bulldozers! After all we've been through together?

ARMANDO. I can't believe what I'm hearing—you all chose this. You could have left—you could have done whatever you wanted.

LORELAILITA. And left Daddy and Tío to rot here? To what? Go to law school? Make lots of money

ARMANDO. Yeah! Sure! And don't tell me I just left—I've been dealing with the legal end of things here since you all took over the restaurant.

LORELAILITA. Yeah… via satellite! You've barely set foot in this place since you went off to your fancy law school.

ARMANDO. It's not my responsibility!

LORELAILITA. Yes—but it is your family.

TÍO COCINERO. Armando—how could you do this to your sisters?

ARMANDO. Listen, Uncle—I've done my part—I've warned you countless times, I've communicated with corporate and tried to find a plan to pay off the debt and get you back on track—but you can't seem to get it together. I've done everything I possibly can to help you—despite the fact that as a child I was never treated like a brother…

AMANDITA. Armando—

ARMANDO. Stop calling me that! My name's not Armando. It's Andy! Andy! Dad just tried to make us sound Hispanic to sell more tacos. Shannonsuela? Lorelailita? THOSE AREN'T NAMES!

And Raymundo isn't our last name either! What? You think my law degree says Armando Raymundo J.D.? Not a chance.

*Shannonsuela can't process what she is feeling. She begins to silently weep.*

TÍO COCINERO. Come on, Armandito—listen to what you're saying, yelling at your sisters. Don't you remember those lazy days of your youth? Sitting by the swimming hole? Popping your dad's famous albondigas into your mouth two at a time?

LORELAILITA. Or how about when it got cold, he'd start our day with the sweetest churros and hot chocolate.

TÍO COCINERO. That's right! The pediatrician begged him to stop, but there was no stopping your father. He loved to see the smiles on your kids' faces when he prepared a new dish. It's what kept him going.

AMANDITA. I'll never forget when he came into our classroom on career day, with you Tío, and turned everyone's lunch into a Cubano.

TÍO COCINERO. We schlepped in six Foreman Grills for that job!

AMANDITA. How he got the PB & Js to taste like ham and mustard I'll never know.

*They fall into a contemplative silence. After a few moments there is a muffled sound. It begins as a cell phone vibration from Amandita's phone, and then starts to crescendo. It hits a violent peak and then lets off a hushed "boing," sounding somewhat like a string breaking. It surprises them.*

… Your app broke my phone.

TÍO COCINERO. So you see, Armandito? There was a method to your father's madness. Without him we would never have been able to open and run this glorious franchise!

*The sisters nod. Armando steps back and takes in the "glorious" establishment.*

ARMANDO. No. I cannot let this insanity continue. I've done everything I possibly can to protect you from this but you couldn't make any concrete changes. You keep talking about Daddy's plan and what Daddy made—but don't you see? Daddy ditched you with this place. He set it up and then he left.

TÍO COCINERO. No, no, Armando, he left to to create, to invent! He took the ripest lemons and the sweetest sugar, mixed it with the finest light beer and…

ARMANDO. You mean Mike's Hard Lemonade? Someone already makes that. Mike already makes that! The bulldozers are outside and they aren't going to wait much longer.

AMANDITA. Wait... Daddy didn't invent Mike's Hard Lemonade?!

ARMANDO. No, Amanda. I'm sorry.

AMANDITA. What about all his "Jamaican" drinks? Jamaican Me Crazy—Jamaican Me Happy—Jamaican Me Spicy?

ARMANDO. *(Putting his arm around her.)* Seagram's.

TÍO COCINERO. Please, Armando. I beg you to reconsider. This place has been a staple of this community for going on forty years. Your father opened one of the first Taco Bells on the East Coast. The sign read "Taco Bell: The El Taqueria." Over the years this place has grown and evolved. We've seen many world events on the TV in the back. "Taco Bell: The Cure for the Common Meal," "Make a Run for the Border," "Spice Up the Night," "Grande Taste, Loco Value," "Yo Quiero Taco Bell," "Think Outside the Bun..."

ARMANDO. Stop listing slogans! It's over!

SHANNONSUELA. How could you?

ARMANDO. I had no choice!

SHANNONSUELA. You could have stayed! You could have helped instead of...

ARMANDO. Instead of what?! Watching this place disintegrate?

SHANNONSUELA. You could have stayed for me at least. You know this is all I have, it's all I'm good at! Where else will they hire someone who can debone a chorizo. Nowhere! Only I can do that for Tío!

TÍO COCINERO. I like a coarse grind.

SHANNONSUELA. I'm useless without this place. I gave my life to keep it going, and now its going to be a parking lot! For a Dollar Barn.

*Shannonsuela starts to sob.*

ARMANDO. Look, Shannonsuela, you could have left... I didn't know how you felt... I just needed to get out...

*Composes himself.*

It's time. My advice: Pack up all of the food and say your goodbyes.

TÍO COCINERO. Oh goodbye dear, beautiful café—where one needn't look far for spicy comfort food and sauce. In these final moments I'm reminded of my famous first invention...

LORELAILITA. Oooh! Tell us Tío.

SHANNONSUELA. Yes—perhaps we will come up with something to save the restaurant. Listen to this, Armando.

> *But he is not listening. He is in the back trying to pack up boxes of napkins, supplies, food, etc. He will be working behind them through the end.*

AMANDITA. Yes!

TÍO COCINERO. Puppy Chili! Ohhh what a delight. I would go to Wendy's and buy several cups of their warm chili. I'd then walk over to Long John Silver's and pick up a few orders of Hush Puppies...

> *He is interrupted by the lights abruptly going off. Blackout. We hear the "breaking string" once more.*

## End of Play

# PROPERTY LIST

Newspaper
Scissors
Smartphone
Boxes of napkins, supplies, food, etc.


# SOUND EFFECTS

Faint whirring of a bulldozer
Cell phone vibration that crescendos into a "breaking string" sound

# NEW PLAYS

★ **A DELICATE SHIP by Anna Ziegler.** A haunting love triangle triggers an unexpected chain of events in this poetic play. In the early stages of a new relationship, Sarah and Sam are lovers happily discovering each other. Sarah and Nate know everything about each other, best of friends since childhood and maybe something more. But when Nate shows up unannounced on Sarah's doorstep, she's left questioning what and who she wants in this humorous and heartbreaking look at love, memory, and the decisions that alter the course of our lives. "Ziegler (who makes origami of time)… digs beneath the laughs, of which there are plenty, to plumb the pain that lurks below." *–Time Out (NY).* [2M, 1W] ISBN: 978-0-8222-3453-1

★ **HAND TO GOD by Robert Askins.** After the death of his father, meek Jason finds an outlet for his anxiety at the Christian Puppet Ministry, in the devoutly religious, relatively quiet small town of Cypress, Texas. Jason's complicated relationships with the town pastor, the school bully, the girl next door, and—most especially—his mother are thrown into upheaval when Jason's puppet, Tyrone, takes on a shocking and dangerously irreverent personality all its own. HAND TO GOD explores the startlingly fragile nature of faith, morality, and the ties that bind us. "HAND TO GOD is so ridiculously raunchy, irreverent and funny it's bound to leave you sore from laughing. Ah, hurts so good." *–NY Daily News.* [3M, 2W] ISBN: 978-0-8222-3292-6

★ **PLATONOV by Anton Chekhov, translated by John Christopher Jones.** PLATONOV is Chekhov's first play, and it went unproduced during his lifetime. Finding himself on a downward spiral fueled by lust and alcohol, Platonov proudly adopts as his motto "speak ill of everything." A shining example of the chaos that reigned in his era, Platonov is a Hamlet whose father was never murdered, a Don Juan who cheats on his wife and his mistress, and the hero of the as-yet unwritten great Russian novel of his day. [9M, 4W] ISBN: 978-0-8222-3343-5

★ **JUDY by Max Posner.** It's the winter of 2040, and the world has changed—but maybe not by much. Timothy's wife has just left him, and he isn't taking it well. His sisters, Tara and Kris, are trying to help him cope while wrestling with their own lives and loves. The three of them seem to spend a lot of time in their basements, and the kids are starting to ask questions. This subterranean comedy explores how one family hangs on when technology fails and communication breaks down. "This smart, disturbing comedy is set…just far enough in the future to be intriguingly weird but close enough to the present to be distressingly familiar… Posner's revelations about this brave new world… waver between the explicit and the mysterious, and each scene… gives us something funny and scary to ponder." *–The New Yorker.* [3M, 3W] ISBN: 978-0-8222-3462-3

**DRAMATISTS PLAY SERVICE, INC.**
**440 Park Avenue South, New York, NY 10016  212-683-8960**
postmaster@dramatists.com  www.dramatists.com